**WITHDRAWN
UTSA Libraries**

Eyewitness Accounts of the American Revolution

Diary of Ezra Green, M.D. from November 1, 1777, to September 27, 1778

The New York Times & Arno Press

Reprinted from a copy in
The State Historical Society of Wisconsin Library

*

Reprint Edition 1971 by Arno Press Inc.

*

LC# 75-140867
ISBN 0-405-01190-3

*

Eyewitness Accounts of the American Revolution, Series III
ISBN for complete set: 0-405-01187-3

*

Manufactured in the United States of America

DIARY

OF

EZRA GREEN, M.D.

Ezra Green
When 100 years old.

DIARY

OF

EZRA GREEN, M.D.,

SURGEON ON BOARD THE CONTINENTAL SHIP-OF-WAR "RANGER,"
UNDER JOHN PAUL JONES, FROM NOVEMBER 1, 1777,
TO SEPTEMBER 27, 1778.

BORN IN 1746; D'ED IN 1847.

WITH

HISTORICAL NOTES AND A BIOGRAPHY,

BY

COMMO. GEO. HENRY PREBLE, U.S.N.,

AND

WALTER C. GREEN.

Reprinted, with Additions, from the HISTORICAL AND GENEALOGICAL REGISTER for January and April, 1875.

BOSTON:
FOR PRIVATE DISTRIBUTION.
1875.

DAVID CLAPP & SON, PRINTERS,
334 Washington Street.

PREFATORY NOTE.

A FEW words may be necessary in respect to the Diary of my father, Dr. Ezra Green, which I am quite sure he never suspected would appear in print before the public eye.

When quite a lad I was, out of curiosity, rummaging over an upper chamber closet, where in promiscuous order were odd volumes,—school books, speeches, sermons, &c.,—when this unpretentious pamphlet turned up in marbled paper-cover. All the particulars of it I had heard my father frequently recount, and hence did not at that early age appreciate its value, and so I gave it to my cousin James D. Green, who, after preserving it with scrupulous care for more than sixty years, has deposited it in the library of the New-England Historic, Genealogical Society, together with important authentic remarks relative to his and my father's progenitors. There this Diary came under the eye of Commodore George Henry Preble, who requested my permission for its publication in the HISTORICAL AND GENEALOGICAL REGISTER, together with such facts as he might gather of my father's public life during five years service as surgeon in the army and navy during the American revolution. To this request I gave my willing assent, promising as a sequel thereto a memoir of his private life.   WALTER C. GREEN.

Boston, Nov. 16, 1874.

BIOGRAPHY OF DR. EZRA GREEN.

I.

HIS PUBLIC CAREER.

By Commodore GEO. HENRY PREBLE, U.S.N.

IN June, 1775, the Sunday after the battle of Bunker Hill, Dr. Ezra Green, in the capacity of surgeon, joined the American army, then under the command of Gen. Artemas Ward, and was stationed with Reed's New-Hampshire regiment on Winter Hill in Charlestown. Here he received the smallpox by inoculation, and was secluded in the hospital at Fresh Pond, Cambridge, for seventeen days, returning to his regiment in camp on Winter Hill the 20th of March, 1776.

After the evacuation of Boston by the British, he left with our army for New-York, going by way of Providence, Norwich and New-London, where they embarked. Having remained in New-York a few weeks, they proceeded up the Hudson to Albany, thence by batteaux to Saratoga; landed, and marched to Lake George; remained about a fortnight; went down Lake George in batteaux, and stopped at Ticonderoga; thence proceeded by Lake Champlain to St. John's; thence to Montreal, and joined Arnold. There the army suffered greatly from sickness. Dr. Green was with the troops which occupied Mount Independence until December, when, on the advance of the British under Sir Guy Carleton, the American forces retreated to Ticonderoga.

The following letter, addressed to his friend Mr. Nath'l Cooper, at Dover, New-Hampshire, graphically describes the situation of the American army at that time.

Ticonderoga, Oct. 30, 1776.

DEAR SIR:

I must beg your pardon for troubling you with so many of my letters, but I am a good deal at leisure, and so lucky an opportunity of conveyance offers, that I can't let it pass without sending you one line or two. Since my last, our Fleet is destroyed, of which I suppose you have heard, but 5 vessels remaining to us out of 16 sail. The engagement began on Friday morning, October 11th, and held out all day. They surrounded our Fleet, but in the night succeeding the engagement they very narrowly and fortunately made their escape and came up towards Crown Point, but were overtaken and attacked again Sunday morning, within about 25 miles of this place. Our men fought bravely, but the enemy were of so much greater force than we had any suspicion of that our little fleet stood no chance; most of the vessels lost were blown up, sunk, or burnt by our own people, they escaping by land. We lost, killed, about 50; taken prisoners, about 100, which are dismissed on parole. The Indians have done us no damage till very lately they waylaid three men, kill'd one, took the other two prisoners, who are sent back on parole. They were treated very kindly by the Indians as well as by the King's troops who were at the time at Crown Point within 15 miles of this place, where they have been ever since the destruction of our Fleet. We have lately been alarm'd several times. On Monday morning last, there was a proper alarm, occasioned by a number of the enemies boats which hove in sight, and a report from a scouting party that the Enemy were moving on; where the Fleet is now, I can't learn, or what is the reason they don't come on I can't conceive. 'Tis thought they are 10 or 12 thousand strong, including Canadians and Indians. We are in a much better situation now than we were fourteen days ago, and the militia are continually coming in. Our sick are recovering, and it is thought we are as ready for them now as ever we shall be. There has been a vast deal of work done since the fight, and we think ourselves in so good a position that we shall be disappointed if they don't attack us. However, I believe they wait for nothing but a fair wind. In my next, I'll tell you more about it. In the meantime I am yours to command.

EZRA GREEN.

My respects to your lady and love to your children.

P. S. I have some thought of leaving the army and joining the navy, provided I can get a berth as surgeon of a good continental ship or a privateer. Should be glad if you would enquire, if you don't know, and send we word what Incouragement is given; and let me know if any ships are fitting out from Portsmouth, and you'll oblige your friend, E. G.

Dr. Green remained with the troops which occupied Mount Independence until they left the position in December, when he returned to Albany, and there left the army and returned to Dover, New-Hampshire. All through the following summer, he was afflicted with fever and ague, but in October, 1777, accepted an appointment as surgeon of the continental ship-of-war Ranger, then fitting out in Portsmouth, N. H., under the command of Capt. John Paul Jones, and nearly ready for sea. They sailed, as his diary shows, on the 1st of November, 1777, for France. The following letter, written to his friend Mr. Cooper, describes the passage out.

On Board the Ranger, Peanbeauf Road,
Dec. 4, 1777.

"SIR:

By a Gentleman who is writing I have an opportunity just to present my respects to yourself and lady, and to inform you of my safe arrival at Peanbeauf 27 miles below Nantz on the 2d of December current, after a passage of 32 days. Our people all in good health and high spirits. We had as good weather as we could wish 'till within a week of our arrival. In the Bay of Biscay we had a very heavy Gale of Wind, but it continued but about 48 hours. Saw but one ship of war, and she was in the chops of the English Channel, with a Fleet under convoy. ⸺ ⸺ I have the happiness to inform you of the Capture of two Brigs, on the 25th and 27th of November, both from Malaga laden with wine and fruit, which on my own and friends account could wish with all my heart were in Portsmouth, New-Hampshire. They were ordered to some part of France, but have not yet heard of their arrival. There is nothing new here. The French say but little about a war, being very intent on getting money. Here are a number of vessels fitting out for America in the trading way. The news of Gen. Burgoine affair got here just before us, and before this time is in all parts of Europe.

I don't expect we shall go from this Place these six weeks, as there is a great deal wanting to be done to the ship before she will go to sea again. It seems probable to me that she will be ordered directly back to America, as soon as may be. In the meantime I am,

With the greatest sincerity & respect,
Your humble servant,
E. GREEN.

Please to present my best regards to Susy[1], & love to your little children, & salutations to all enquiring Friends.

Mr. Nathaniel Cooper, of Dover,
New-Hampshire,
New-England.

Dr. Green continued in the Ranger until her return to Portsmouth in October, 1778, when he left her, and returned to Dover.

When the Ranger was refitted in the following spring, under the command of his friend, Capt. T. Simpson, he rejoined her as surgeon, and sailed in her on a cruise in company with the Warren, 32 guns, Commodore J. B. Hopkins, and Queen of France, 28, Capt. J. Olney; the latter a French ship, which had been purchased at Nantes for the American government.

While on this cruise, in March, they captured a privateer schooner of 14 guns, and on the 6th of April the schooner Hibernia, of 8 guns and 45 men, and the next morning, off Cape Henry, six more of a fleet of nine vessels, viz.: the ship Jason, Capt. Porterfield, 20 guns, 150 men; ship Maria, letter of marque, 16 guns, 80 men, cargo of flour, &c.; and brigs Prince Frederick, Patriot, Bachelors John, and schooner Chance, all laden with stores for the British army. Among the prisoners taken was a Colonel Campbell, and twenty-three army officers of lesser rank, on their way to join their regiments at the south.[2] All these vessels were brought into Portsmouth, N. H., three weeks after the squadron sailed from thence.

On another cruise, the Ranger, still commanded by Simpson, in company with the Providence, 28, Commodore A. Whipple, and Queen of France, 28, Capt. J. P. Rathburn,[3] on the 17th of July, 1779, when on the Banks of Newfoundland, fell in with the Jamaica fleet, homeward bound, consisting of one hundred and fifty sail,

---

[1] This was Susannah Hayes, whom he subsequently married.
[2] Emmons's History U. S. Navy, 1776–1853.
[3] The Queen of France, Providence and Ranger, all three under the same commanders, were sunk at Charleston, S. C., May 12, 1780, by the British Squadron, after that city had surrendered to the forces under Sir Henry Clinton.

convoyed by a ship-of-the-line, and several cruisers, and succeeded in capturing eleven large ships, of seven to eight hundred tons, three of which were re-taken; but seven of them, whose cargoes were estimated to be worth $1,000,000, were brought safely into Boston. All Boston was alarmed at the sight of the little continental squadron and its prizes,—ten large ships standing directly into the harbor,—believing them to be a British fleet. The buildings were covered with spectators. The cargoes, consisting of rum, sugar, logwood, pimento, &c., were delivered one half to the government and one half to the captors.[1]

On his return from this successful cruise, Dr. Green resigned his position as surgeon of the Ranger in favor of Dr. Parker, of Exeter, and returned to Dover.

In 1780 he sailed on another cruise in the Alexander, Captain Mitchell, 14 guns, but they accomplished nothing. In 1781, the vessel having been fitted up as a letter of marque, under Captain Simpson, he went in her to Fredericksburg, Virginia, and they took thence a load of tobacco to l'Orient in France. He returned in the Alexander to the United States in the autumn of that year, which concluded his revolutionary services.

II.

DR. GREEN'S PRIVATE LIFE AND CHARACTER.

By WALTER C. GREEN.

My father, Dr. Ezra Green, was born in Malden, Mass., June 17, 1746, and, after he was graduated at Harvard College in 1765, he commenced the study of medicine and surgery with Dr. Sprague, of Malden, finishing his course with Dr. Fisher, of Newburyport. He then went to Dover, New-Hampshire, to reside, in 1767, where he was in successful practice up to his appointment as surgeon in the army. Dr. Green's five years service in the army and navy I need not describe, it having been already narrated by Commodore Preble.

About the same time that Dr. Green went to reside in Dover, his friend the Rev. Jeremy Belknap, from Boston, was by unanimous vote invited there and ordained minister of the Congregational Society on a salary of £150, payable semi-annually, and there he preached for eighteen years. This small pittance being inadequate for the support of himself, his wife, two sons and two daughters, he asked a dismissal, and returning to Boston, he was soon settled as minister over the Federal Street Society, and there remained until his greatly lamented death, June 20, 1798, at the early age of 55 years. Dr. Belknap was my father's next-door neighbor, and the close intimacy so early commenced between the two families, never abated during their lives.

[1] The Rev. Dr. Lothrop's Centennial Sermon in Dover, N. H., June 28, 1846 (Appendix)

When Dr. Green and the Rev. Mr. Belknap went to Dover, my dear mother was eight years of age, and being of a lively, pleasant disposition and quick apprehension, with an ardent fondness for books and study, she early enlisted their kind offices in the direction of her various studies; and to them she was largely indebted for her excellent education.

On the 13th of December, 1778, my father was married to my mother, Susannah Hayes, of Dover, by the Rev. Jeremy Belknap. This fortunate union remained unbroken, save for his absence during the remainder of his service in the navy, until it was severed by her death,—a period of fifty-seven years.

In a letter from on board the Ranger dated March 12, 1779, Dr. Green wrote to his then young married wife : "I never felt so uneasy on account of your absence. I pray we may not long be separated from each other, but as Providence seems to have pointed out this to me as a duty, I desire to pursue it cheerfully and with good courage, and I know you would not wish me to turn or look back; and I wish you all the happiness of this world and that to come." As soon as he had discharged the duty here mentioned, that is, on the termination of the revolutionary war, Dr. Green relinquished his medical practice to his friend and successor, Dr. Jacob Kittredge, to whom he gave his surgical instruments, books and medicines, and then commenced a mercantile business.

Early after this he was made post-master in Dover, which office he voluntarily resigned after several years of faithful duty.

Dr. Green was made deacon of the First Congregational Society in Dover, and was a most devout, unfailing attendant on all Sunday or week day religious services, despite the adverse weather of severest cold or snow of winter, or scorching heat of summer. My father's religious education gave to his early and middle life a degree of asceticism that controlled his thoughts and conduct; but from this in his later years, with a wider range of religious and theological information, and with greater experience and reflection, he happily emerged into broader views of the truths of Christianity. These gave him fresh vitality, and added a more gentle influence and sweetness to his character.

In the year 1827, Dr. Green, with many others of similar religious belief, withdrew from the First Congregational Church, and formed the First Unitarian or Second Congregational Society in Dover. In the affairs of the new society, though nearly 80 years of age, he took an active and prominent part, and especially in erecting, during the year 1828, a large commodious church, in which the Rev. Samuel Kirkland Lothrop soon after was called to preach as the first pastor of the society; presiding in that ministry with satisfactory zeal and fidelity for five years, until 1834, when he was called away to a wider field of usefulness, to the pastorship of the

Brattle Square Church in Boston, where he happily officiates to this late day with no diminution of ardor and faith.

Dr. Green and family were fond of friendly social intercourse, and his doors were ever open and largely frequented by the refined and cultivated persons of both sexes, who appreciated their society and liberal hospitality.

In the various affairs of the town, he took a lively interest, and under his charge the first school-house was built; and for educational and religious purposes, the dissemination of the Scriptures at home and abroad, and support of the ministry, he was always a willing contributor.

From time to time he served as selectman, or as surveyor of the highways and by-ways, and now and then as moderator at the town-meetings, where the clashing parties of Federalists and Democrats met, with passionate party feelings, which at times raged with scarce controllable fury.

From active mercantile business in 1811, he sought that domestic quietude with his devoted wife and family he so fondly cherished, and there he largely indulged his taste in reading to their ever attentive ears. He was no hum-drum reader, but with a clear voice and superior elocutionary powers he rendered his various readings pleasingly attractive, and this was his fondest daily enjoyment, up to the very verge of his prolonged years.

My dear mother had but a feeble constitution, yet I never knew her depressed in spirits. Her well-stored, retentive memory made her society attractive to the old and young who frequented her house; and as a wife and mother, she was in all her duties watchfully diligent and greatly endeared by her family. Her life was that of a liberal Christian, and she awaited her exit from this world with patient resignation, and in the happy belief of an immediate entrance into a future life of endless duration and happiness; and thus she passed away, on the 3d of April, 1836, in the 77th year of her age.

During those early times it was the prevailing fashion, whatever the hour of a friendly call, to invite the guest to imbibe as he might prefer from the several potations before him. The custom was a pernicious one, and when the temperance societies sprung up, Dr. Green, though always a most temperate person, was the first to enter his name on the list of "total abstinents," not from the least necessary restrictive requirement on his part, but because he hoped it might prove an efficient example for many of his fellow-townsmen, who were more or less demoralized by this habitual indulgence.

He had no craving desire for official position or for public notoriety. He was, however, honored by several governors of the state with a commission as justice of the peace, and was also chosen one of the delegates at large, and chairman of the state convention for the adoption of the constitution of the United States. His vote gave a majority in its favor, an event of profound importance for New-Hampshire, to which the other assenting states were looking for this hoped for result, with no small doubt and distrust of feeling.

He had a fond taste for horticulture, and in his garden it was his daily enjoyment to spend a few hours in healthful exercise, where he gloried over his various fruits and delicacies. From his wife's farm of 150 acres, four miles from town, most of the staple necessaries of life were produced, so that at his table, where there was no needless waste, there was a sufficiency to satisfy the keenest appetite or most dainty palate. His garden at one time had more than thirty peach trees, most of which were killed by an untimely snow-storm in June, when they were in full blossom. The few which escaped during my boyhood I well remember for their luscious flavor.

He was no less fond of pomology, and during the fall season he took me behind him on his horse Whitey to the farm to assist in carrying the implements for ingrafting his young thrifty apple orchard, and with eager eyes I watched the sound selected branch from which with fine saw he lopped off the upper portion. Next with mallet and chisel midway the stalk was cleft for the wedge-cut scion's insertion where the two barks met to catch the up flowing sap in spring. Then with trowel the plastic clay was overlaid to hold firm the scions against the rude blasts of winter, and then the flaxen tow was wound around, and last of all a bandage deftly fastened, and all so artistically done, as in a few years well repaid him with its ample fruitage. Several trees were grafted with scions cut from an aged tree in Massachusetts, the bark nearly destroyed by the wood-peckers, and hence its name of "Pecker-Apple." It attained a large size, resembling the well-known Baldwin, though firmer and handsomer; and when ripe in mid-winter, it was with its crisp golden pulp and juicy flavor the most delicious apple I have ever eaten.

Dr. Green was an ardent patriot and Federalist, a brave and consistent champion of that independence he had helped to win, and a zealous advocate for that constitution he had aided to establish. From early life to the last he was an opponent of the institution of slavery, and predicted that sooner or later the free and slave states would be involved in a bitter controversy on that account. That he was spared the realization of his fears, was a mercy to his sensitive heart.

In his mode of life he aimed at no ostentatious show. Polite and affable in his deportment, he won the respect due to courteous manners.

In personal appearance and contour of face, he was not unlike Gen. Washington, for whom he was often taken while in the army. In stature he was six feet three inches tall and proportionately large in frame; and whether walking or sitting, he always maintained a very erect position. The woodcut engraving which accompanies this sketch represents Dr. Green at the age of fifty-five years, and is a very perfect outline likeness. The steel engraved portrait is taken from a rather indistinct daguerreotype likeness when he was one hundred years of age. He had a sound, vigorous constitution, strengthened and preserved by uniform temperate habits, daily physical exercise, early hours for retirement, and rising with the opening day. At the age of 82 years he fell and broke his thigh bone where it entered its socket; and little did he or his physician believe that at his advanced age it would ever unite, as it did after several months confinement to his bed; so that in the course of time, with the aid of crutch or cane, he was enabled to hobble about his house and garden, and occasionally to attend church.

Ten years more had nearly elapsed, when another more serious accident befel him. From an early morning stroll in front of his house, he came in doors, and standing by the window reading, was suddenly prostrated backward to the floor, seemingly, to him, by a violent blow on his cranium, and so wrenching his spinal column, as deprived him ever after of all power of locomotion. Happily this accident was unattended with pain, and there in his cosey easy chair, with books, papers, &c. around him, his days and years flew apace without weariness or complaint, and with that sweet serenity of mind and calm christian patience which won the most devotioned care and affectionate love of his two only surviving daughters.

From his personal friends, he had frequent social visits, and from strangers not a few, from far and near, attracted by his venerable age, or a desire to hear him recount his varied experience during our revolutionary war. Groups too of merry children, for whom he had a kindly fondness, came often with tasteful flowers to greet him. Such indeed was his uniform gentleness of disposition, and lively interest in all public and domestic affairs, that he left questionable evidence on the minds of not a few strangers, as to the extreme old age attributed to him.

Here, in conclusion, I will add that, on learning my dear father's indisposition, I hastened to see him, and found him suffering somewhat, as it seemed, from the effects of a cold and cough. To gratify me he took some homœopathic pellets I recommended, smilingly remarking that such an infinitesimal potion could neither kill nor cure. Finding himself the next morning much relieved, he exclaimed that that was not what he desired, "for it has been my daily prayer the last year to my Heavenly Father, to take me to himself, and I believe he has kept me here a year longer, for my ceaseless importunity." Whereat I asked, have you not enjoyed your usual good health and happy intercourse with your devoted daughters and friends? O yes! that I have, and every worldly comfort and enjoyment I desire, but now I long to depart. Like the late renowned Mrs. Mary Somerville, of England, he dreaded the possibility of his physical powers outliving his mental faculties; and then said, "what an incubus I should be to my loving daughters, who would then wish me in my grave."

Happily was it that he was exempt from all those fretful, fractious feelings to which aged people are occasionally subject. Such was his universal cheerful temperament and mental activity, that his death to his idolizing daughters was no less grievous than that of a darling child to a fond mother; and so it was, that this eminently good and venerable man's prayer was soon after my visit indulged, and on July 25, 1847, he expired at the very advanced age of 101 years and 28 days, retaining to his last hour a clear unclouded mind, and with the full faith and confiding hope of entering a future world of progressive improvement and happiness.

On the one hundredth anniversary of Dr. Green's birth-day, the 28th of June, 1846, his former friend and pastor, the Rev. Samuel K. Lothrop, of Boston, preached in Dover a commemorative discourse[1] on this event, and from its appendix I make the following extract:—

Dr. Green is still able to employ himself with books for several hours every day. He reads the papers, and keeps himself well informed upon all public affairs, and retains his interest in them. As an evidence of the declaration that "the intellect and the heart have been slightly touched by time," I am permitted to publish the following extracts from a record, made in my journal, of an interesting interview had with him after service on the Sunday on which the sermon was preached. I had said that he was so well and strong that perhaps his life would still be prolonged some years; to which he replied—" I know not how long I may live. Death was always a very solemn and affecting thing to me. When a young man nothing affected or impressed me so much as a funeral. It has been so through life and is so now. I contemplate death with awe. It is a solemn thing to die, to exchange worlds, to enter upon an untried, spiritual, eternal state of being, of which we can form no adequate conceptions. To appear before an omniscient God, to account for the deeds done in the body, *all* of them, through a *long* life, is a solemn thing; I feel it to be so—I have always felt

[1] THE CONSOLATIONS OF OLD AGE. | A | Sermon | Preached at the | First Unitarian Church, in Dover, N. H | On the 28th of June, 1846, | Being the One Hundredth Birth-day | of | Ezra Green, M.D. | The Oldest Living Graduate of Harvard College. | By S. K. Lothrop, | Pastor of the Church in Brattle Square, Boston: | 1846. | Eastburn's Press. ! [8vo. pp. 25.]

it. But I thank God that I am able to contemplate him as my Father in Heaven. Through Jesus Christ, the mediator, I have hope in his mercy, and a perfect trust in his paternal goodness." * * * *

These observations, and others in a similar strain, were made spontaneously, with pauses in which he seemed to be collecting his thoughts, but with only a single question put to him on my part. I publish them, not on account of the particular religious opinions which they express, but for the evidence they afford of the unabated vigor and activity of his intellect at the age of an hundred years. I have given very nearly his exact words. He was much affected during the utterance of these sentiments, and evidently spoke from the bottom of an earnest and sincere heart. The interview was exceedingly interesting, and left on those present the impression that he was ripe for the Kingdom of Heaven, and that an old age surrounded by so many comforts, with the intellect and the heart so little impaired, was not so sad and gloomy a period as we sometimes imagine.

In June, 1846, he received the following letter from Daniel Webster:

WASHINGTON, June 17, 1846.

MY DEAR SIR:—I hope you remember me at that period of my life, when I was in the habit of attending the Courts at Dover, and when I had the pleasure of enjoying your society and hospitality.

And I hope that in subsequent life I have made some efforts which you have approved, for the maintenance of those political principles to which, as a friend and follower of Washington, you have ever been attached, and which I have heard you so often and so intelligently defend. This is the day* on which you complete the hundredth year of your age. Will you allow me, therefore, to greet you, to-day, with a respectful and friendly letter, congratulating you on the degree of strength, mental and bodily, which Providence allows you to enjoy, so far beyond the lot of man, and tendering to you my cordial and affectionate good wishes for your continued health and happiness. I send you a copy of a speech lately made by me in the senate, and remain, dear sir,

Your friend and obedient servant,

Dr. Ezra Green.   DANIEL WEBSTER.

To my cousin the Hon. James D. Green, of Cambridge, Mass., I am indebted for the following authentic annals from his manuscript volume, in the library of the New-England Historic, Genealogical Society, in Boston, relative to his and my father's earliest progenitors.

Dr. Green's earliest ancestor who came from England to this country, was:

1. JAMES[1] GREEN, yeoman, 24 years. He was an inhabitant of Charlestown, 1634, and admitted freeman of the colony in 1647, purchasing lands and settling in "Mystic Fields," since called Malden. He died March 29, 1687, aged 77 years, leaving a widow and two sons, John and James. After a proper provision for his widow and son James, he willed his "lands and housing thereon" to his son John.

* Mr. Webster fixed the date according to the "old style" of reckoning, which explains the apparent discrepancy between his statement and the date named in Dr. Lothrop's sermon.

2. JOHN² (*James¹*), the eldest son of James, was born about 1650 and died at the age of 59, leaving a widow, three daughters and one son, Samuel, to whom, after providing for his widow and daughters, he by will gave all his lands in Malden and Charlestown " to him and his heirs forever."

3. SAMUEL³ (*John,² James¹*), who was born in 1679, was a representative of the town in the general court in 1742. His wife died at the age of 72, and he died February 21, 1761, at the age of 82, leaving four sons: James, John, Timothy and Ezra, and one daughter, Mary Dana. To his beloved son Ezra, he by will gave all the remainder and residue of his real and personal estate, he paying his debts, funeral expenses and the various bequests to his other children and granddaughters.

4. EZRA⁴ (*Samuel,³ John,² James¹*), was born in 1714, and married Sarah Hutchinson, who died July 7, 1741, at the age of 26 years. His second wife, Eunice Burrell, of Lynn, died October 20, 1760, aged 47, leaving two sons, Ezra and Bernard. For his third wife, he married Mary Vinton, by whom he had one son, Aaron. Said Ezra Green was deacon of the church in Malden, selectman and representative in the general court during the years of 1760, '61 and '62. He died April 28, 1768, at the age of 54 years. By his will, after providing for his beloved widow Mary, he gave to his son Ezra twenty acres of land in Chelsea, and about five acres near " Penny Ferry," apart from what he had paid for his collegiate and medical education, and the gift of a horse, which he deemed equivalent to the homestead, real and personal (except what he had disposed of to his son Aaron, besides his collegiate educational expenses), which he bequeathed to his son Bernard, making as it did the fifth generation, and embracing more than two hundred years since its first purchase by James Green in 1610.

Dr. Green was in his second year's naval service, when, by the Rev. Jeremy Belknap, he was married to Susanna Hayes in the twentieth year of her age. She was then reputed to have been quite handsome and a great favorite with all her acquaintance. She had a delicate and petite figure, nut-brown hair, shading bright hazel eyes that lit up her regular cut features with a winning expression, which played over a soft transparent complexion, lovely as a fresh-blown rose.

Her father's will, making his estate reversionary in the event of his daughter's decease without issue, happily placed her and her husband in no such unpleasant dilemma; for in the brief time of nineteen years, thirteen children were born to them, viz.:

    i. EUNICE, b. July 1, 1780; d. Oct. 7, 1782.
    ii. REUBEN HAYES, b. Aug. 20, 1783.
    iii. CHARLES, b. March 26, 1785; d. April 5, 1854.
    iv. DEBORAH SHACKFORD, b. March 20, 1787; d. May 7, 1860.
    v. SARAH, b. Oct. 19, 1788; d. Nov. 2, 1874.
    vi. SAMUEL, b. Jan. 4, 1790; d. Jan. 23, 1791.
    vii. MARTHA, b. July 13, 1791; d. Nov. 25, 1792.
    viii. EUNICE, b. Oct. 8, 1792; d. May 25, 1839.
    ix. A DAUGHTER, b. July 15, 1794; still-born.
    x. MARTHA, b. June 9, 1795; d. Aug. 3, 1795.
    xi. A SON, b. April 27, 1796; still-born.
    xii. SAMUEL, b. Oct. 5, 1797; d. Nov. 3, 1823.
    xiii. WALTER COOPER, b. July 1, 1799.

My mother's earliest paternal ancestor* in America,

---

* I am mainly indebted for the annals of my mother's paternal ancestry to John R. Ham, M.D., of Dover, N. H.

1. JOHN[1] HAYES, is said to have emigrated from Scotland about 1680, and settled in Dover, New-Hampshire. He had a grant of land in 1693. By his wife Mary Horn, he had seven sons and three daughters, viz.:

2. i. JOHN, b. 1686.
   ii. PETER.
   iii. REUBEN.
   iv. ICHABOD, b. March 13, 1691–2.
   v. SAMUEL, b. March 16, 1694–5.
   vi. WILLIAM, b. Sept. 6, 1698.
   vii. BENJAMIN, b. ———, 1700.
   viii. A DAUGHTER, m. Phipps.
   ix. A DAUGHTER, m. Ambrose.
   x. A DAUGHTER.

2. JOHN[2] (John[1]), married Mrs. Tomson, and lived at Tole-End, four miles from Dover corner. He was a deacon of the First Congregational Society in Dover. They had eight children, viz.:

   i. ANN, b. June 3, 1718.
3. ii. REUBEN, b. May 8, 1720; d. 1762.
   iii. JOSEPH, b. March 15, 1722.
   iv. BENJAMIN, b. March 6, 1723.
   v. MEHITABEL, b. Dec. 11, 1725.
   vi. JOHN, went to North Yarmouth, Maine, to reside.
   vii. ELIJAH, went to Berwick, Maine.
   viii. ICHABOD, went to Berwick, Maine.

3. REUBEN[3] (John,[2] John[1]), was born May 8, 1720. He lived at Tole-End and married Abigail Shackford, by whom he had only one child, viz.:

   i. SUSANNA, b. March 23, 1759.

Reuben Hayes died in 1762, at the early age of 42 years, and by his will, after a liberal provision for his wife Abigail, he gave all the residue of his estate, real and personal, to his only child Susanna Hayes, consisting of his farm of 150 acres at Tole-End, with this reservation that, in case "his said daughter Susanna, at her decease, should leave no issue of her body lawfully begotten surviving, then my will is that, my whole estate that shall then be remaining, both real and personal, shall revert and be divided among my four Brethren, namely, Benjamin, John, Ichabod and Elijah Hayes."

DIARY OF DR. EZRA GREEN.

Portsmouth Road, Nov. 1st, 1777. *Saturday.*—Between the hours of 8 & 9 this morning weigh'd anchor and proceeded to Sea with a moderate breeze, before night lost sight of the American shore.
Sunday, Nov. 2nd.—A very fine morning and a favorable wind, all well on board—except some few who are a little Seasick.
Friday, Nov. 7th.—A strong gale at Northwest which carrys us 10 knots.
Thursday, Nov. 13th.—About seven this morning saw a sail on our lee Bow distant about 2 Leagues, gave chase and spoke her about 12 o'clock, a Brig from Carolina bound for Bordeaux with several Tory Passengers on Board, among whom were Hartley the Organist & his wife.
Friday, Nov. 14th.—This Morning at 5 o'clock came up a severe Thunder Storm from the southwest.
Saturday, 15th.—Last evening came on a gale of wind which increas'd till about 3 this morning when it began to abate, in the hight of the gale a sail was seen under our lee Quarter, hove too till she came up, a Schooner from St. Peters bound to Bordeaux.
Sunday, 16th.—A fresh Breeze, and high Sea from the late Gale, about 10 o'clock our tiller Rope broke by which we were in great Danger of the Consequences of the Ship's broaching to.
Wednesday, 19th.—About six this morning saw a Sail under our lee Quarter, gave Chase or rather bore away till we came within

---

[1] The Ranger 18, was built 1777, on Langdon's Island, Portsmouth Harbor, by order of Congress, under the direction of Colonel James Hackett.
On the 14th of June, 1777, Congress *Resolved*, That Capt. John Paul Jones be appointed to command the ship Ranger, and under date Philadelphia, June 18, 1777, the marine committee write to him, "You are appointed to the command of the Ranger, lately built at Portsmouth. Col. Whipple, the bearer of this, carries with him the resolves of Congress appointing you to this command, and authorizing him, Col. Langdon, and you to appoint the other commissioned as well as warrant officers necessary for this ship, and he has with him blank commissions and warrants for this purpose."
Though great diligence was used by Jones in equipping the Ranger, she was not ready to proceed on her destination until the middle of October. Twenty-six guns had been provided for the ship, but Jones exercised great judgment in mounting only eighteen on her, as he considered from her size and slight construction, that she would be more serviceable with eighteen than with a greater number. The following extracts from his letter to the marine committee, dated Oct. 29, 1777, two days before sailing, gives a lively idea of the difficulties he had to contend with, and the poverty of our resources. "With all my industry I could not get a single suit of sails completed until the 20th current. Since that time winds and weather have laid me under the necessity of continuing in port. At this time it blows a very heavy gale from the northeast. The ship with difficulty rides it out, with yards and topmasts struck and whole cables ahead. When it clears up I expect the wind from the northwest, and shall not fail to embrace it, although I have not now a spare sail nor materials to make one. Some of those I have are made of hissings. I never before had such disagreeable service to perform, as that which I have now accomplished and of which another will claim the credit as well as the profit. However, in doing my utmost I am sensible that I have done no more than my duty."
Thus imperfectly equipped, having a very good crew, but "only thirty gallons of rum," as Jones laments, for them to drink on the passage, the Ranger sailed from Portsmouth on the 1st of November, 1777.—*Mackenzie's Life of Paul Jones.*

about a mile of Her found Her to be a large Ship standing Our course clued up Our Courses and hawl'd Our wind—got ready for Action she standing on her course close to the wind, wore Ship when it was too late, continued the chase till night and lost Her.

Saturday, Nov. 22nd.—At nine o'clock this morning saw a Sail on our weather Beam—little wind; One of Our People fell from the Chains but was saved by a Rope's End handed Him.

Sunday, Nov. 23rd.—Early in the morning saw a Sail supposed to be the same we saw yesterday, came up with and made a Prize of—about 8 o'clock, a Brig laden with fruit and wine from Malaga bound to Yarmouth, Riches Comm^r.—She is called the Mary—there are no less than six sail in sight at this Time.

Monday, Nov. 24th.—Spoke a Schooner from Malaga bound to Liverpool vessel and Cargo owned by a Portugal Merch^t.

Tuesday, 25th.—Last night spoke a Ship & Snow bound to France,—and are now chasing a vessel under Our lee Bow, at 11 at night came up with & made a Prize of the Brig George from Malaga bound to London laden with fruit and wine, she was commanded by Bulfinch.

Wednesday, 26th.—Early in the morning gave chase to a Brig under our lee Bow, but were obliged to give over Chase on seeing a very large Ship to windward with several other Sail in Company she appeared to be standing athwart us, about 2 she hove too with a Fleet of 13 Sail of Ships & Brigs at 2 Leagues Distance, clewed up Our Courses & stopp'd our Ship's way expecting every minute when she would come down upon us about 4 she stood on her Course, we made sail close to the wind with a design to cut off a Brig which could not keep up with the Convoy, lost her in the night.

Thursday, 27.—A fresh gale from the S. W. in the afternoon vear'd a Barrel of Beef astern for the Brig, Sea running High she carelessly ran upon our Larboard Quarter but did no other Damage than breaking our Driver Boom—at 10 at Night saw several Sail spoke one of them found them all to be Dutch Daugers.

Saturday, 29th.—A very heavy gale, hove too at night in the Bay of Biscay 60 Leagues distant from Land.

Sunday, 30th.—Fine weather and a strong wind in the night hove too and sounded in 80 Fathom water.

Monday, Dec. 1.—Saw Land from mast Head at 10 in the morning, with fine weather,

Tuesday, Dec. 2nd.—Ran in for the Land with a fine moderate Breeze, narrowly escap'd running on a Sand through want of a Pilot and arrived all in good spirits at Peanbeauf on the River Loire and came to anchor in the evening.

Wednesday, 3rd.—Wrote a Letter to Capt. Shackford at L'Orient and inclos'd one to my very good friend Cooper—favour'd by Capt. Mutchemore.[1]

---

[1] The letter to his friend Cooper is given in the Memoir.

Friday, Dec. 5th.—The Prize Brig Mary arrived here safe—went to Nantez with Capt. Simpson arriv'd at 9 in the Evening this is a very considerable City distant 10 Leagues from Penbeauf am told there are 12 Parishes in Nantes in one of which are 30,000 Souls.
Saturday, Dec. 6.—Went to the Tragedy but it was to me in an unknown Tongue, was not much pleased or entertained, however the Musick was good.
Sunday, Dec. 7.—Returned to Peanbeauf, and on board the Ranger.
Friday, 13 Feb.—Set sail for Quiberon Bay M^r. Williams & Brother on board, in company with us Brig Independence, anchored in the Bay about six in the Evening, 4 Ships of the Line besides Frigates in the Bay.
Saturday, 14th Feby.—Very Squaly weather, came to Sail at 4 o'clock P. M. saluted the french Admiral & rec'd nine guns in return this is the first salute ever pay'd the American flagg.
Sunday, 15th Feb'y.—Brig Independence saluted the french Flagg which was return'd.[1]
Wednesday, 25th Feb'y.—Fleet got underway and left us at anchor contrary to Expectations, about 12 O'clock it being very windy we came to sail, ran out of the Bay without a Pilot, attempted to the Northward of Belisle, but did not succeed, put back hoping to run into the Bay again, but could not weather the Rocks. in the midst of our Trouble having narrowly escap'd over setting the Ship, were alarm'd with the cry of Fire—after all our endeavours to procure a Pilot were in vain, & night coming on, bore away and ran out to the Leward of the Island, very squaly still.
Thursday, 26.—Arrived in Quiberon-Bay again the Evening after a short but very tedious & unprofitable Cruize.
Tuesday, March 3rd.—Weigh'd anchor and came to Sail in fine weather & smooth water, sail'd along the Coast about 25 Leagues and came to anchor in a small Bay near a small village called Benodett, had a curious Adventure with a french Pilot who came on Board to pilot the Ship but would not be compell'd to take charge of her.

[1] Jones, in his letter to the naval committee, dated Feb. 22, 1778, reporting this important recognition of our flag, says:—
" I am happy to have it in my power to congratulate you on my having seen the American flag, for the first time, recognized in the fullest and completest manner by the flag of France. I was off this bay [Quiberon Bay] on the 13th inst., and sent my boat in the next day to know if the Admiral would return my salute. He answered that he would return to me as the senior continental officer in Europe, the same salute as he was authorized to return to an Admiral of Holland, or any other republic, which was four guns less than the salute given. I hesitated at this, *for I had demanded gun for gun.*
" Therefore I anchored in the entrance of the Bay at a distance from the French fleet; but after a very particular inquiry, on the 14th, finding that he really told the truth, I was induced to accept his offer, the more *as it was an acknowledgment of American Independence.*
" The wind being contrary and blowing hard, it was after sunset before the Ranger was near enough to salute La Motte Piquet with thirteen guns, which he returned with nine. However, to put the matter beyond a doubt, I did not suffer the Independence to salute until the next morning, when I sent word to the Admiral that I would sail through his fleet in the Brig and would salute him in open day. He was exceedingly pleasant, and returned the compliment also with nine guns."

Thursday, March 5th.—Went with Joseph Ratcliff to Pontlably and procured good lodgings for Him supposing the Eruption (which came out last night) to be Small Pox—we were treated with great respect as we were Americans, were waited on near half a mile to the Boat and on parting gave them 3 Cheers which was answered with vive Le Congres.

Friday, March 6th.—This morning (being fine weather) came to sail, in the morning went through of Passage Duroi; saw a large Ship to the leward which we thought was a Frigate & the same we saw yesterday: She fail'd in attempting to get through the Passage and stood off.

Saturday, March 7th.—Came to anchor in Baldavids Bay not far from the River of Brest.

Sunday, March 8th.—Weigh'd and beat up towards Brest came too in Camaritt's Bay 4 Leagues from Brest.

[At Brest] *Tuesday, March 10th.*—Last night eight of our People took the Cutter and went on shore and ran off leaving the Boat on the Rocks.

Friday, March 13th.—Seven of eight Deserters were bro't back under guard & confined in Irons.

Saturday, 14th March.—Went to Brest with Capt. Jones & Lt. Simpson; had a slight view of the Fortifications, Shipping, and Dock-Yards—return'd in the Evening.

Sunday, 15th.—I had the pleasure of entertaining the Commissaries Lady & two Sisters on Board the Ranger.

Wednesday, 18th.—Last night died after a lingering Illness for more than three weeks Willm Reading—His remains were decently interr'd about 11 oclock A.M.—P.M. the Ladies came to pay Capt. Jones a visit as he was absent when they pay'd us the first Visit.

Monday, 23rd March.—Got under way and ran up to Brest; saluted the Admiral, rec'd the news of L^d. Stormont's having left Paris on receiving a copy of the Treaty with America.

Thursday, 2nd April.—Got up anchor pay'd the french flagg another Salute rec'd. 11 for 13—One of our Seamen narrowly escap'd drowning; when the Ship was coming to sail was turned off from the Spritsail Yard the Ship went over Him, but He was luckily taken up by the Man who was in the Cutter which was veard astern arriv'd at Camaritt about 5 O'clock P.M. and came to anchor.

Friday, 3rd April.—Our Ship being laid on Shore for cleaning I went with our Pilot & L^t. Wallingsford to take a view of the New Fort which is building on an Eminence at the distance of three miles from Camaritt.

Sunday, 5 April.—Attempted to get out to sea with the Fortuna of 36 guns but were oblig'd to return to Brest.

Wednesday, 8th.—Made a second Attempt to get out & fail'd.

Friday, 10th.—About 5 O'clock P.M. came to Sail in Company with the Frigate [Fortuna]—were detained by the Cutter which was sent after Sand to Camaritt.

Saturday, 12th.[1]—Fine weather but no Convoy to be seen, about 10 in the morning saw a sail to windward which prov'd quite contrary to our fears to be the Fortuna—we were all ready for action when she came alongside of us.

Monday, 14th.—Our Convoy left us, sooner than Capt. Jones Expected which He resented but could not prevent.

Tuesday, 15 April.—Early in the morning saw a Brig under our Lee Bow, about 8 o'clock spoke her : from Ostend to Galway laden with Flaxseed took the People their Baggage &c. on board scuttled and left Her.[2]

Wednesday, 16th.—Made some part of Ireland in the morning suppos'd to be the high Land of Dungarvin.

Thursday 17th.—Saw a Ship in the afternoon under our lee Bow, at Sun's setting spoke Her—a Ship of about 350 Tons from London for Dublin laden with Hemp Iron Porter &c &c. ordered her to Brest.[3]

Saturday, 19th.—Made a warm attempt to take a Cutter mounting 8 Guns, she slipped through Our Fingers, had the Captain have permitted the Marines to fire on them when they first came under our lee Quarter might have taken Her with great Ease.

Sunday, 20th.—In the morning near the Isle of Man sunk a schooner laden with Barley & Oats about 60 Tons burthen from some part of Scotland, in the Evening sunk a Sloop in ballast from Ireland.[4]

Monday, 21st.—Bore down for Belfast Loch, took a fishing Boat with 4 Men in sight of a Ship at anchor they informed Us that she was a Man of war of 20 guns ; we made sail and stood off about an Hour, when the Capt. ordered the ship to be put about in order to go in and cut her out, but the wind blowing fresh and the people unwilling to undertake it we stood off and on till midnight when the People consenting and the wind having lulled a little we stood into the River but it being somewhat Dark did not drop our Anchor so as to lay her along side, therefore were oblig'd to cut and run out, which we were very lucky in effecting.[4]

[1] Saturday was the 11th April, 1778. From this entry to that on Friday the 24th, there is a discrepancy of one day between the day of the week and the month.

[2] Jones, in his report to the American commissioners, written on the 27th of May, from Brest, says : "On the 14th I took a Brigantine between Scilly and Cape Clear, bound for Ostend, with a cargo of flaxseed for Ireland, sunk her, and proceeded into St. George's Channel."

[3] Jones calls this ship the Lord Chatham, and says that she was captured almost within sight of her port.

[4] Jones says with regard to these affairs : "On the 18th, in Glentine bay, on the south coast of Scotland, I met with a revenue wherry ; it being the common practice of these vessels to board merchant ships, the Ranger then having no external appearance of war, it was expected that this rover would come alongside. I was, however, mistaken; for though the men were at their quarters, yet this vessel outsailed the Ranger, and got clear in spite of a severe cannonade.

" The next morning (19th) off the Mull of Galloway, I found myself so near a Scotch Coasting Schooner, loaded with barley, that I could not avoid sinking her. Understanding that there were ten or twelve sail of merchant ships, besides a Tender brigantine with a number of impressed men on board, at anchor in Lochran in Scotland, I thought this enterprise worthy my attention ; but the wind, which at the first would have served equally well to sail in or out of the Loch, shifted in a hard squall, so as to blow almost directly in, with an appearance of bad weather. I was therefore obliged to abandon my project.

" Seeing a cutter off the lee bow steering for the Clyde, I gave chase, in hopes of cutting her off ; but finding my endeavors ineffectual, I pursued no further than the Rock of Ailson. In the evening I fell in with a sloop from Dublin, which I sunk."

Tuesday, 22nd.—Stood off and on all Day with a design to make another Trial if the wind lull'd at night there being no signs of more moderate weather wore ship and stood back towards Galway Mull— Our people very much fatigued.

Wednesday, 23rd.[1]—Weather somewhat more moderate & our people a little recruited, Our enterprising Capt. with about 30 men went on shore about 11 P.M. with a Design to fire the Town of Whitehaven.[2]

[1] Jones in his report says: "The 21st, being near Carrickfergus, a fishing boat came off which I detained. I saw a ship at anchor in the road, which I was informed by the fishermen was the British ship of war Drake, of twenty guns. I determined to attack her in the night; my plan was to overlay her cable, and to fall upon her bow, so as to have all her decks open and exposed to our musquetry, &c.; at the same time, it was my intention to have secured the enemy by grapplings, so that, had they cut their cables, they would not have attained any advantage. The wind was high, and unfortunately the anchor was not let go as soon as the order was given, so that the Ranger was brought to upon the enemy's quarters at the distance of half a cable's length. We had made no warlike appearance, of course had given no alarm; this determined me to cut immediately, which might appear as if the cable had parted, and at the same time enable me, after making a tack out of the Loch, to return with the same prospect of advantage which I had at first. I was however prevented from returning, as I with difficulty weathered the light-house on the lee-side of the Loch, and as the gale increased. The weather now became so very stormy and severe, and the sea ran so high, that I was obliged to take shelter under the south shore of Scotland."

[2] Jones's account of this important affair is as follows:—

"The 22d introduced fair weather, though the three kingdoms were, as far as the eye could reach, covered with snow. I now resolved once more to attempt Whitehaven; but the wind became very light, so that the ship would not in proper time approach so near as I had intended. At midnight I left the ship with two boats and thirty-one volunteers; when we reached the outer pier the day began to dawn; I would not, however, abandon my enterprise, but despatched one boat under the direction of Mr. Hill and Lieut. Wallingford, with the necessary combustibles to set fire to the shipping on the north side of the harbor, while I went with the other party to attempt the south side. I was successful in scaling the walls and spiking up all the cannon in the first fort; finding the sentinels shut up in the guard house, they were secured without being hurt. Having fixed sentinels, I now took with me one man only (Mr. Green), and spiked up all the cannon in the southern fort, distant from the others a quarter of a mile.

"On my return from this business, I naturally expected to see the fire of the ships on the north side, as well as to find my own party with every thing in readiness to set fire to the shipping on the south; instead of this, I found the boat under the direction of Mr. Hill and Mr. Wallingford returned, and the party in some confusion, their light having burnt out at the instant when it became necessary. By the strangest fatality, my own party were in the same situation, the candles being all burnt out. The day too came on apace, yet I would by no means retract while any hopes of success remained. Having again placed sentinels, a light was obtained at a house disjoined from the town, and a fire was kindled in the steerage of a large ship, which was surrounded by at least one hundred and fifty others, chiefly from two to four hundred tons burden, and lying side by side, aground unsurrounded by the water. There were, besides, from seventy to a hundred large ships on the north arm of the harbor, aground clear of the water, and divided from the rest only by a stone pier of a ship's height. I should (would) have kindled fires in other places if the time had permitted; as it did not, our care was to prevent the one kindled from being easily extinguished. After some search, a barrel of tar was found, and poured into the flames, which now ascended from all the hatchways. The inhabitants began to appear in thousands, and individuals ran hastily towards us. I stood between them and the ship on fire, with a pistol in my hand, and ordered them to retire, which they did with precipitation. The flames had already caught in the rigging, and began to ascend the mainmast; the sun was a full hour's march above the horizon, and as sleep no longer ruled the world, it was time to retire. We re-embarked without opposition, having released a number of prisoners, as our boats could not carry them. After all my people had embarked, I stood upon the pier for a considerable space, yet no person advanced; I saw all the eminences around the town covered with the amazed inhabitants.

"When we had rowed to a considerable distance from the shore, the English began to run in vast numbers to their forts; their disappointments may easily be imagined when they found, I suppose, at least thirty heavy cannon rendered useless. At length, however, they began to fire, having, as I apprehend, either brought down ship's guns, or used one or two cannon which lay on the beach at the foot of the walls, dismounted, and which had not been spiked. They fired with no direction, and the shot falling short of the boats, instead of doing us any damage afforded some diversion; which my people could not help

Thursday, 24th.—After watching the night and all the morning till broad day light in expectation of seeing the smoke of the Town and Shipping (ascend as the smoke of a Furnace) began to fear that Our People had fallen into the Enemies Hands; however about half an hour after sun rise we discovered two small Boats at a great Distance coming out of the Rivers mouth, and clouds of smoke arising from the Shipping, soon after we saw them fire on the Boats from the Shore, but most of the Cannon being spiked up by our People they could do but very little the Boats were soon out of their Reach and came along-side with 3 prisoners for one left behind.

The same Day crossed over to the other side of the Bay to the Mull of Galway Capt. Jones with Lt. Wallingsford and about 12 Men went on shore [at St. Mary's Isle] with design to take L^d. Selkirk, Prisoner. As he was not at Home and no man in the House, for the sake of his Lady & her Company they came off without doing any further Damage than plundering Him of Plate to the amount of (as near as I can judge) 160lb. weight of Silver.[1]

Friday, 24th.—Early in the morning our Capt. proposed making a second attempt to cut out the Ship in Caracfergus, which was now within a small Distance, the People both officers & men discovr'd gread unwillingness to make the attempt. Capt. Jones notwithstanding declar'd publickly his determination to go in, in short it seem'd impossible to avoid it for the Tide & what little wind there was, had

showing, by discharging their pistols, &c. in return of the salute. Had it been possible to have landed a few hours sooner, my success would have been complete. Not a single ship, out of more than two hundred, could possibly have escaped, and all the world would not have been able to save the town. What was done, however, is sufficient to show, that not all their boasted navy can protect their own coasts; and that the scenes of distress, which they have occasioned in America, may soon be brought home to their own door. One of my people was missing; and must, I fear, have fallen into the enemy's hands after our departure. I was pleased that in this business we neither killed or wounded any person. I brought off three prisoners as a *sample.*"

In a memorial to congress Jones says, " His first object was to secure an exchange of prisoners in Europe, and his second to put an end, by one good fire in England, of shipping, to all the burnings in America," and he expresses the opinion, that had his officers in the Providence and Alfred been with him in the Ranger, two hundred and fifty to three hundred large ships at Whitehaven would have been laid in ashes. In the Ranger's logbook the man left on shore is named David Smith, and it was thought he remained on shore voluntarily, and that under the name of Freeman, he gave information at several houses that fire had been set to the ships.

[1] *The attempted Seizure of the Earl of Selkirk,* &c.—On the 8th of May following, Jones wrote from Brest to the Countess of Selkirk, with regard to the taking of this plate, that he was obliged to command while he did not approve of the act, and thus expresses the object of the expedition.

." Knowing Lord Selkirk's interest with the King, and esteeming as I do his private character, I wished to make him the happy instrument of alleviating the horrors of a hopeless captivity, when the brave are overpowered and made prisoners of war," and " it was my intention to have taken him on board the Ranger, and to have detained him until, through this means, a general and fair exchange of prisoners, as well in Europe as in America, had been effected. When I was informed, by some men whom I met at the landing, that his Lordship was absent, I walked back to my boat, determined to leave the Island. By the way, however, some officers who were with me, could not forbear expressing their discontent, observing that, in America, no delicacy was shown by the English, who took away all sorts of moveable property—setting fire not only to towns, and to the houses of the rich, without distinction, but not even sparing the wretched hamlets and milch cows of the poor and helpless, at the approach of an inclement winter. That party had been with me the same morning at Whitehaven; some complaisance, therefore, was their due. I had but a moment to think how I might gratify them, and at the same time do your ladyship the imperceptably carry'd us in so far that there was very little chance for an Escape, and now which was about sun-rise we saw the Ship with Her Sails loos'd and had nothing to do but to get ready for Action Our People at the same Time discovering the greatest readiness to engage Her. When she [the Sloop of war Drake] came out at 11 almost Calm about 12 Saw a Boat coming from the Ship which we Decoy'd and took on board a Midshipman & 5 Men; there being a light Breeze of Wind & understanding by the People from the Ship that she was coming Out to us; clung our wind and stood out under easy sail till 4 O'clock, P.M. & hove too for Her, she came up about 6 and hailed after the usual Compliments were pass'd we wore Ship and gave her a whole broad side, without receiving a Shot: the Action continued till 5 minutes after seven very warm when her 2 Commanding Officers being the one Capt. Brurdon killed & the other Lt. Dobbs mortally wounded and about 20 of Her Men disabled and the Ships Rigging Sails &c. very much damaged they were oblig'd to give her up by the wave of the Hat & a call for Quarters for having the Second Time cut away their Ensign staff they had no Colours to Strike.

least injury. I charged two officers to permit none of the seamen to enter the house, or to hurt anything about it,—to treat you, Madam, with the utmost respect, to accept of the plate which was offered, and to come away without making a search, or demanding any thing else.

"I am induced to believe I was punctually obeyed; since I am informed, that the plate which they brought away is far short of the quantity expressed in the inventory which accompanied it. I have gratified my men ;.and when the plate is sold I shall become the purchaser, and will gratify my own feelings by restoring it to you, by such conveyance as you shall please to direct."

Lord Selkirk wrote a letter in reply, intimating that he would accept the return of the plate, if made by order of congress, 'but not if redeemed by individual generosity. The letter, however, was detained in the general post office, London, and returned to the earl, who requested a gentleman to communicate the cause of its miscarriage and its tenor orally to Dr. Franklin, who at once informed Jones of the substances of the communication. Meanwhile the plate had fallen into the hands of the prize agents, and it was not until the beginning of 1780, and by the purchase of seventeen twentieths of it, that Jones obtained possession of it. When he had succeeded in effecting this object, he wrote again to the Countess of Selkirk; but his voyage to America retarded its delivery until 1784. It was eventually returned in the same condition in which it had been removed, and Lord Selkirk subsequently acknowledged, as the following extracts from his letter to Paul Jones, dated *London, August* 4, 1789, the unwearied pains Jones had taken to secure its restoration.

"I received the letter you wrote to me at the time you sent off my plate, in order for restoring it. Had I known where to direct a letter to you, at the time it arrived in Scotland, I would then have wrote you. * * * Notwithstanding all the precaution you took for the easy and uninterrupted conveyance of the plate, yet it met with considerable delays; first at Calais, next at Dover, then at London; however, it at last arrived at Dumfries, and I dare say quite safe, though as yet I have not seen it, being then in Edinburgh."
"I intended to have put an article in the newspapers about your having returned it * * and on all occasions both now and formerly, I have done you the justice to tell, that you made an offer of returning the plate very soon after your return to Brest; and although you yourself was not at my house, but remained at the shore with your boat, that yet you had your officers and men in such extraordinary good discipline, that your having given them the strictest orders to behave well, to do no injury of any kind, to make no search, but only to bring off what plate was given them; that in reality they did exactly as ordered, and that not one man offered to stir from his post on the outside of the house, nor entered the doors, nor said an uncivil word; that the two officers staid not a quarter of an hour in the parlor and the butler's pantry, while the butler got the plate together, behaved politely, and asked for nothing but the plate, and instantly marched their men off in regular order, and that both officers and men behaved in all respects so well, that it would have done credit to the best disciplined troops whatever."

Lost on our side,—Lt. Wallingsford[1] killed by a musket shot in the head. John W. Dangle by a double H^d. shot cut in two in the Fore Top.
Wounded,—Pierce Powers lost his right Hand, & his left badly wounded. James Falls by a musket shot through the Shoulder. Thos. Taylor lost his little Finger by a musket shot at the wheel.

Saturday, 25th.—Very pleasant and almost Calm a fine Opportunity for repairing and fitting for Sea from on board the Drake buried the Remains of Capt. Burdon with the Honors of war— spoke a Brigg from white Haven of about 300 Tons commanded by Capt. More, put a Prize Master and Hands on Board Her: at 12 we were not far from the place of action about 2 Oclock P.M. having a light Breeze sent away the Fishing Boat's crew with a present of Money 17 Guineas and the Drakes Main Sail & M^n. Top Sail; in the Evening committed the Body of Lt. Wallingsford to the deep with the Honours due to so brave an Officer.

Monday, 4th May.—Died of his wounds and the same day were decently buried the Remains of Nathl. Wells of Portsmouth, America.

Thursday, May 7th.—Arrived at Brest with the Ship Drake in Company.

May 9th, Saturday.—Sent on Shore to the Hospital Pierce Powers, James Falls & Thos. Taylor from the Ranger at the same Time sent from the Drake 13 Prisoners.

Sunday, 10th May.—Arrived here the Prize Brig Patience.

Wednesday, 13th.—Sent to the Hospital John Mott a Prisoner taken in the Drake.

Friday, 29 May.—Drew a petition in behalf of my good Friend Simpson now in goal in Brest which was sign'd by Lt. Hall M^r. Cullam and myself & sent on shore to the Office in order to go to the Commissioners at Paris.

Thursday, 18th June.—Rec'd the news of an Engagement between a French & English Frigate not far from Morleaux, the French Frig. was ordered out to Adm^l Byron to speak, she refus'd to Obey therefore were fired on by the Eng— the action began about half past 4 on the afternoon of yesterday and continued 5 hours, though the Eng^h struck they were prevented bringing her off by Adml Byron's Squadron 12 sail of the Line besides Frigates— the French Frigate lost 1 Lt. 1 officer of Marines and 38 men killed, and about 60 wounded.

Thursday, 2nd July.—Had the company of Col Frazier & M^r. Pringle to Dine, afternoon went with them & Lieut^s. Simpson & Hall on board the Britaigne of 110 Guns & 1400 Men were treated with the greatest civility & Respect from all on Board.

---

[1] Lieut. Wallingsford's christian name was Samuel. Doct. Green told his son he was a lieutenant of marines. His son George Washington Wallingford, born in Somersworth, N. H.; and an infant two months old at the time of his father's death, was a distinguished lawyer of Maine. (See Willis's *Law and Lawyers of Main*, pp. 252, 256.)

Friday, 3rd July.—This day arrived a Schooner called the Spy from New London with Dispatches from Congress.

Saturday, July 4th.—This being the Anniversary of American Independence, was observed as such Our Ship was dressed 13 guns discharg'd at 10 O'clock; At undressing 13 more; on drinking the Duke de Chartre's Health 9 guns were fired; a number of Patriotic Toast were drank; and universal Joy was diffused throughout the whole Ship's company.

Wednesday, July 8th.—This day the Fleet sail'd from this Place about 33 sail of the Line besides Frigates.

Thursday, 9th.—This Day arrived here a Brig from Carolina with Rice—no news C. Ray.

Friday, July 10th.—This Day the Lively Ship of war was brought into this harbour. On her refusing to comply with the commands of Capt. of the Frigate by which she was taken, she receiv'd a broadside from the Cannon & the fire from the Swivels & musketry both from below and aloft, which was returned by 3 guns when she struck. Her loss was about 20 kill'd & 40 wounded most of whom are since dead.

Friday, July 17th.—This day was brought in here the prize Cutter Alert of 12 guns the same which took the Lexington Brig of 14 guns Johnson Comm^r. She was taken by a Frigate.

Sunday, 28 June last were brought in here Two Cutters from Guernsey taken by Frigate Snow.

Wednesday, 22 July.—Rec'd the news of C. De Astangs arrival in Boston.

Monday, July 27th.—This day Thomas Simpson Esq^1 came on board with orders to take command of the Ranger; to the joy and Satisfaction of the whole Ships company.

[1] This change of commanders was at Jones's request on the 4th of July. He wrote to the commissioners at Paris,—" When Congress thought proper to order me to France it was proposed that the Ranger should remain under my direction, not be commanded by a Lieutenant. And as the French ministry have now in contemplation plans which promise honor to the American flag, the Ranger might be very useful in carrying them into execution. Lieut. Simpson has certainly behaved amiss; yet I can forgive, as well as resent; and upon his making a proper concession, I will with your approbation not only forgive the past, but leave him the command of the Ranger. By this means, and by some little promotions and attentions, I hope to be able to satisfy the Ranger's crew, so that they will postpone their return as long as the service may require."

On the 13th of August, he wrote the commissioners from Brest, "I have been five days in this place since my return from Passy, during which time I have neither seen nor heard from Lieut. Simpson; but Mr. Hill, who was last winter at Passy, and who sailed with me from Nantes, informs me truly, that it is generally reported in the Ranger, and of course throughout the French fleet and on shore, that I am turned out of the service; that you gentlemen have given Mr. Simpson my place, with a Captain's commission, and that my letter to you of the 16th of July, was involuntary on my part, and in obedience only to your orders." That these reports prevail, is not an idle conjecture, but a melancholy fact. Therefore, I beseech you; I demand of you to afford me redress—redress by a court martial," &c. On the 15th of August, he wrote Capt. Abraham Whipple, then at Brest, requesting that a court martial might be summoned for the trial of Simpson, but Capt. Whipple writes him, explaining the impossibility of forming a court, and expressing it as his opinion, that as he had given up the parole of Simpson, in the most ample manner without asking for concessions, nothing could be done.

Lieut. Simpson sailed in the Ranger for America. On the 30th of August, Jones's friend Mr. Williams, writing to him from Nantes, in relation to the pending sale of the Drake, said, "I am sorry your affair with Lieut. Simpson was not settled with mutual satisfaction. If

Tuesday, July 28th.—This Day arrived from the Lamp [illegible] of 60 guns, with news of an Engagement between the Fleets.
Wednesday, July 29th.—Last night arrived a 74 This Day arrived the Fleet, excepting 1 of 80 1 of 60 and 1 Frigate, which they say parted from them in the Fog—they appear to have sustained no very considerable Damage in the late Fight.
Saturday, Augt. 8th.—Sent to the Hospital three of the Drake's People viz: Jno Wilkinson Pilot John Colbert & John Rickets Seamen.
Sunday, Augt 9th.—Sent to the Hospital Joseph Larcher a Prisoner from ye Drake.
Saturday 15.—Last night arrived Here the Barton & Providence, Whipple & Tucker from Nantes.
Thursday, 20th Augt.—Moved down in Company with the Providence & Boston Frigates, about four Leagues & came too, to give the People an Opportunity of expending their Prize Money. I had a very Fatiguing Time up to Brest on Business for Capt. Simpson and the widow of my deceas'd Friend Lt. Wallingford for whom I bought 32 Crowns worth.
Friday, 21st.—Very little wind this morning came to Sail & got down about 2 Leagues & anchored. At 3 P. M. came to Sail again and ran out with a fine Breeze.
Saturday, 22.—Very fine weather in the morning saw a Sail ahead were order'd by our Commodore to give chase came up with Her about 5 P. M. a Spanish Snow bound to Haver du Grace.
Sunday, 23rd Aug.—Chased a Dutchman all Day.
Monday, 24.—Spoke Brig call'd the Sally from London laden

he was not gone, I should answer his charge of falsehood with the following paragraph of his own letter to me, of the 1st of August, to mine, which you say he calls false, viz : ' I recollect my telling you when at Brest, that if Capt. Jones had condescended to have made any inquiry, or permitted him to speak to me on the matter of my confinement, I was ready to give him any satisfaction consonant with truth.' It is strange he should recollect this when he wrote me the letter, and forget it again when he told Mr. Hill it was false. Lieut. Simpson's letter to me is in very respectful terms, and I wrote him a letter of thanks in return. He desired me to present his respects to you, and tell you that 'your recommendation to the commissioners, which I mentioned, would, with any services you had done him, be ever remembered with gratitude.'"

The Ranger arrived safe in America, and Lieut. Simpson was continued in command of her until she was destroyed at Charleston, after which we hear no more of him in the naval service.

In February following, the commissioners addressed a letter to Jones, stating, that as his separation from the Ranger, and the appointment of Lieut. Simpson to the command of her would be liable to misrepresentation, they certified that his leaving her was by their consent, at the express request of M. de Sartine, who informed them that he had occasion to employ Jones in some public service; that Simpson was appointed to the command by the consent of Jones, who had released him from the arrest he had placed him under; that Jones's rank in the navy was not prejudiced by his leaving the Ranger; and that his commission remained in full force.

In a letter addressed to Robert Morris, dated Oct. 10, 1783, Jones says, he "received orders to proceed to Europe, to command the great frigate building at Amsterdam, for the U. S.; then called the Indien, and since the South Carolina,"—and " it was proposed that he should proceed to France in a ship belonging to that kingdom ; but, some difficulties arising, the sloop of war Ranger of 18 guns was put under his command for that service, and to serve afterwards as a tender to the Indien, but political reasons defeated the plan, and after seeing the commissioners in Paris, agreeably to their order to consult on the means of carrying it into execution, he returned to Nantes and resumed the command of the Ranger."

with Provisions, Beef Flour & Butter, 150 Tons Burthen. Sent her to America. Lat. 45.32 Long. 10.22.

Wednesday, September 2nd.—Being in chase in Latt. 47.21 Long. 27.24 at 3 P. M. carry'd away Our fore Top Mast and Main Top gall. Mast.

Wednesday, Sept. 9th.—Latt. 46.7 Long. 36.29. Took a Brig called the Friends from Granada bound to Glasco with Rum & Cotton about 100 Tons Burden. 10 Bags Cotton 134 Puncheons Rum.

Wednesday, 16th Septr. in Latt. 45.45 Long. 41.47 Took a Snow from Newfoundland Laden with Fish 150 Tons Burthen.

Thursday 17th.—7 Morn gave chase to a large Ship to windward as far as we could see them from Top of mast head 7 in the Evening, came very near them but night coming on lost sight of them.

Friday, 25th September.—In Latt. 44.45 had soundings on the Banks of Newfoundland in 82 Fathoms, Foggy.

Sunday, 27th Sept.—Spoke a Brig from Amsterdam called the William Robert Stonehouse Comm^r bound to Boston the same Day saw an Island of Ice at a Distance which had the appearance of a Lofty Sail we pass'd within a League of it to windward. The Brig is Laden with Tea and Cordage.